The Resume Doctor

An Rx for Resume Writing and Interviewing Skills

Leslie L. Jackson

Dedication

This book is dedicated to everyone who knows they are great and have the skills, but need help translating those skills to potential employers.

Acknowledgements

———— ⟨∞⟩ ————

I would like to thank God for blessing me with the gift of administration and giving me the vision for this book. I would like to thank everyone who trusted me with their skills and work history, and allowed me to present them at their best on paper, which garnered them an interview, a job, or their greatest salary to date. Thank you so much for your feedback.

TABLE OF CONTENTS

Prologue

For as long as I can remember I wanted to be a secretary. Growing up I watched television shows with smart and sassy secretaries like Mrs. Malone from WKRP in Cincinnati played by Loni Anderson; Carol Hester from Bob Newhart Show, and who could forget, Ms. Hathaway from the Beverly Hillbillies.

I envisioned myself travelling all over the world by private plane, jet-setting across the globe to international meetings with my wealthy and influential boss! And I was weirdly excited at hearing the words, "The boss will see you now."

My dream was technically realized when I joined the United States Air Force. I scored rather high on the Administrative portion of the Armed Services Vocational Aptitude Battery (ASVAB) test and was selected for my dream career. I graduated from high school in June and by October, I was in the Air Force.

I spent the next twenty-one years, nine months, and eighteen days as an Air Force Administrator and yes, I was privileged to travel all over the United States and several countries on behalf of my "wealthy and influential boss," Uncle Sam.

The image of fancy leather seating was replaced by red-netted jump seats; international meetings became international deployments, and "The boss will see you now" was replaced with a military reporting statement. Most days I loved every minute of being in the military and the people I worked with.

Twenty-one years seem like a long time when you are eighteen years old, but I have been retired over ten years now. I know it was just a blip on the screen of my life. I met some amazing people along the way, a few became life-long friends.

As a military administrator, I learned marketable skills, was trained for leadership and management, gained two college degrees with no student loan debt incurred, and earned a well-deserved retirement! Lastly, I was able to translate my military administrative skills into the civilian employment sector.

Since retiring from active duty military service, I have worked as an Administrator in the civilian sector for a corporation with annual retail sales of $2.6B; an international government agency servicing thirty countries and a Fortune 500 company.

I also have experience being unemployed. I have willingly left the traditional workforce to pursue entrepreneurial opportunities. I have worked as a contractor and became unemployed when the contract ended, and I have been terminated due to a company-wide war on overhead.

I know what it feels like to be notified fifteen minutes before the end of your shift that today will be your last day. I know what it is like to begin again and it is my duty to share my insight with you.

I have a one-hundred-percent verifiable success rate to date with resume writing, meaning if I write the resume, there is a one- hundred-percent chance you will get the interview (and the job).

Because I cannot personally write one million resumes for each of you, I am writing this book with the goal of helping you get your foot in the door, literally, to be interviewed! But what if you have no work history? I am glad you asked.

When You Have
No Work History

"No experience is experience
that needs to be translated."
~ Leslie L. Jackson

When my kids were babies, I would explain everything I did. "I am putting your red sock on your left foot." When they were old enough to follow me around the house, I put them to work which they thought was fun. By the time they figured it out, it was too late, and they were already contributing members of the household. That is work experience.

When teenagers discover or are told that money does not grow on trees and they will need to work outside the home to earn money for the extras in life that they deem necessities, they can pull work experience from their everyday life. This also applies to homemakers or stay-at-home parents entering or returning to the work force.

Some examples of translating work experience: If you have raked leaves, taken out the garbage, or washed dishes, you have done physical and manual labor. If you have cleaned a room and put away toys or dishes, you have experience organizing and stocking items. If you have asked your family what they want for dinner, cooked, and served it, you can wait tables.

If you have budgeted for your family vacation, and planned where you will stay, and what you will do, you have financial and travel experience. Are you always on time? Then you are punctual. These are all qualities desired from employees. These are entry-level employment skills.

We all have experience, it just needs to be translated into another context, or in this case, a professional resume to take us to the next level we desire to go. Are you ready? Okay, great! Let us begin.

A Standout Resume

*"You never get a second chance
to make a first impression."*
~ Andrew Grant

The above quote has never been truer than when it comes to submitting your resume. Your resume is often the first introduction to the company you are trying to gain employment with. You want it to make a lasting impression.

On average, hiring managers spend six seconds to two minutes viewing each resume. Yes, you read that correctly, six seconds to two minutes! Commercial software programs scan documents for pre-selected buzzwords which narrow down the number of resumes to be reviewed by the hiring manager.

According to a 2019 statistic, there are a minimum of two-hundred fifty resumes submitted for every advertised corporate employment opportunity, and only two percent of those received are reviewed by hiring managers.

So how do you make your resume stand out? I am glad you asked. In the pages that follow, I will share my proven resume techniques for developing a resume and cover letter that gets you elevated to an interview. For your resume to stand out, it should be three things: clear, concise, and compatible.

Clear. I previously mentioned that hiring managers spend six seconds to two minutes reviewing resumes. This means they do not have time to read through paragraphs of adjectives stating how wonderful you are, especially paragraphs that do not pertain to the work experience they are looking for.

Make it easy for the hiring manager to choose you. Your resume should clearly and *only* identify the verifiable skills that you have which match the employment opportunity. Verifiable means that if they were to call your former supervisor, he or she will confirm that you have the skills to complete the task proficiently.

Your sentence structure or bullet statements should be no more than three lines describing the skill and how you used it to save the company time/man-hours, resources, and/or money.

It is not enough to state that you have the skill, what sets you apart is your ability to apply the skill accurately, to advance the mission, vision, values, goals, and objections of the organization. Again, only include skills and experience that pertain to the job you are applying to.

Concise. Again, six seconds to two minutes of resume review time. You do not have a lot of time to catch the eye of the hiring manager. I recommend a one-page* resume with one-inch margins all around.

Choose a font that translates well electronically and on paper when printed out. An Internet search for "resume font for (insert current year)" will suffice.

If you have a lengthy work history, you will need to condense it down to the most significant accomplishments that relate to the employment opportunity you are seeking. You can expound on your work experience once you gain the interview.

Your resume must look professional. Too many visual accents on the page can detract from your actual skills. Section titles are a larger font than the body; bolded, and underlined, however refrain from excessive borders, too much underlining and capitalization. You want your resume to stand out, not put off.

I do not recommend putting a photo on your resume. You want to be judged solely on your knowledge, skills, and abilities. You can however, use a small monogram or logo. Keep it simple.

Compatible. Your resume should show the hiring manager in six seconds to two minutes that you have the skills the company is looking for. Your skills should be current and relevant to the position you are applying to.

I have been an Administrator for over thirty years however, it would not benefit me to list skills from thirty years ago. That is my point. List only the skills that are current and relevant to the employment opportunity. Carefully reading the position description will help you determine relevancy.

Read the position description and highlight the experience the hiring manager is looking for. Next, read your resume and highlight your work experience that relates to the requested skills. If your skills match up with what the hiring manger is looking for, you are probably a good candidate for the position.

There may be times when you have the skills but need help translating them into key words from the employment ad. An example of this would be a military person transitioning into the civilian work force.

When using acronyms I recommend stating the proper name of the item the first time it is used, then putting the acronym in parenthesis, and then using the acronym going forward if necessary.

And speaking of acronyms, please do not assume the hiring manager knows what your acronym means. For example, PT in the military world stands for physical training, in the medical world, physical therapy or patient, and in the workforce, PT can mean part-time. When in doubt spell it out.

Professional Summary, Headings, and Information

"You can't build a reputation on what you're going to do."
~ Confucius

Whether you title your heading "Career Summary" or "Professional Summary," the first paragraph of your resume is where you shine and peak the hiring manager's interest to keep reading!

The Summary tells the hiring manager some details about your work experience, and why they should hire you, or at least select you for an interview. The Summary highlights your expertise, sharing what you have to offer and what qualifies you for the position.

The remaining headings are interchangeable. Carefully reading the employment ad will help you decide what to put first. The headings that can be used are: Career Highlights, Employment History, Technical Skills, Academic Qualifications (Education), and Certifications.

After the Summary, you want to share your Career Highlights by identifying three to five bullet statements from your most recent job history, that feature exceptional performance.

Career Highlights should identify something you drafted, orchestrated, developed, or accomplished, that saved the company time, man-hours, resources, or all the above.

Examples include: If you were hand-picked for a project, or if you were pivotal in an inspection or audit that received the highest rating, it should be presented here. If you trained your peers and they went on to get promoted or receive recognition, it should be identified in Career Highlights.

Other Career Highlight items include development of a process or procedure that was incorporated beyond your department, to the rest of the company. Next is your Employment History.

Your Employment History should list your job title, the company name, city, and state where you worked, and the month and year you worked at the company.

I recommend a maximum of ten years of work history go on your resume. This helps you keep it to one page* and gives you the opportunity to expound on work history and experience outside the ten years, during the actual interview.

Under Technical Skills is where you put your typing, keyboarding, and/or 10-key speed, MS Office proficiency (certified test scores are a plus), and any other software related programs that are relevant to the position you are applying to. Any specialized training could go here as well.

Academic Qualifications also known as education goes next, starting with the most recent degree obtained. List the type of degree, education major, the school, city and state, and the year graduated or anticipated graduation date.

If you have multiple higher learning degrees, list only those that relate to the employment opportunity you are applying to. Lastly, list any certifications you have obtained such as A+ or Network+ certification.

The "references available upon request" in the footnotes is optional. For employment references, I recommend you have a prepared page that lists at least one supervisory reference, a peer reference, and a personal reference.

Some companies now ask for two of each type of reference so be prepared. Make sure that your references know you are seeking employment and have a copy of your current resume handy, in case they are called upon to verify your employment information and/or speak to your professional character and work habits.

You want to have ***zero*** spelling or grammatical errors when applying to an employment opportunity. Do not rely solely on the spell check feature. Read the resume forward and backward (*literally*), take a break, then read it again. Once your resume is complete and error-free, you can move on to the cover letter.

* If you are applying to a Federal Government position (usajobs.gov), it is accepted and expected for your Curriculum Vitae (CV)/resume to be more than one page.

Use a chronological work history that relates to the position with the most recent job first. Include job titles, starting and end dates, annual salary, hours worked per week, specific bullets about your accomplishments and level of experience. You can also include relevant volunteer and community work.

Cover Letter

"Allow myself to introduce...myself."
~ Austin Powers

The cover letter is a brief formal introduction from you to the company and announces your resume while affirming your interest in the employment opportunity.

The cover letter should emphasize the skills that qualify you for the job, state your most recent significant accomplishment that pertains to the position, and if possible, use an accomplishment that is not listed in your resume under Career Highlights.

The Cover Letter should be addressed to the hiring manager by name if you know the person's name. You may also address the cover letter "To Whom It May Concern" if there is no name available.

Once these two documents are complete you can upload them to the company website via computer, or fax them to the hiring manager or Human Resources (HR) office. You can also go the old-fashioned route and "snail mail" your documents to the company through the US Postal Service or via FedEx.

If you are applying to multiple positions, keep an interview binder or folder with sheet protectors inside. Place a copy of the employment ad and the resume you submitted inside the sheet protector back to back. Be sure to write the date of submission somewhere on the page.

When the interview call comes in, having these documents together will help you quickly identify the company and locate the resume you submitted.

An interview binder will also help if you have to do any follow-up interviews, or if it has been a while since you heard from the interviewer and you need to follow-up on the interview/hiring progress, and reaffirm your interest in the position.

Some employment hiring can take two months or longer. You may be contacted to confirm that you are still interested in the position you applied to. If you have the option to continue waiting, be patient for the right opportunity.

The Call to Interview

"They like me, they really like me." ~ Sally Field

Congratulations, you have been selected for an interview! The moment you have been waiting for has finally arrived! The interview is where you go into greater detail about your knowledge, skills, and abilities that pertain to the employment opportunity.

When the call comes in give yourself one or two days to prepare for the interview, especially if you have not yet completed your research on the company.

Make sure you write down the time, date, and interview location. Ask if there are any special entry/access instructions, and whether there will be anyone to greet or escort you into the interview location. Finally, confirm a contact number for the interviewer in case of emergency.

Repeat the interview information back to the caller to confirm everything you wrote down is correct. Also, ask whether the interview will be one-on-one or a panel of interviewers. Once the call has ended and you have completed your happy dance, it is time to prepare for the interview.

What Not to Wear

"Nothing succeeds like the appearance of success."
~ Chris Lasch

Whether you are interviewing for a warehouse position or a CEO, you should always dress your best. Personal grooming is more than the clothes you wear, it is your overall head-to-toe appearance. Here are some suggestions to ensure your appearance compliments your resume.

1. Personal Hygiene. Shower or bathe and use deodorant the morning of the interview. This may seem like common sense however, I have interviewed a

person who smelled like they had closed the pub the night before.

If you suffer from nervous perspiration or anxiety sweat, make sure you bring personal hygiene wipes and extra deodorant. Floss and brush your teeth and use mouthwash.

2. Hair and Nails. Make sure your hair is clean and neat. It is best to pull your hair back from your face and ensure any bangs do not cover your eyes during the interview.

    Make sure your nails are clean and free of dirt underneath, and if they are polished, wear clear, a complimentary nude or natural shade. If you struggle to pick up coins or objects with your nails, they may be too long for a professional workplace.

If you will be working in a professional setting such as medical, food service, or a conservative office, try to keep your nails to a length that does not impede your ability to do your job.

3. Makeup and Perfume. Natural looks with nude eyeshadows and lip colors work best. It is best not to wear perfume or colognes during interviews.

Many people suffer from respiratory issues like asthma and allergies and perfumes and colognes can cause flare-ups in small interview spaces. If you must wear fragrance, spray it in the air one to two times and walk through the fragrance mist.

4. Jewelry and Hosiery. Keep jewelry to a minimum. Small pearl, silver, gold, or diamond-studded pierced or clip-on earrings, one ring on each hand, a watch, and a pearl or other necklace that lies flat is more than enough.

If you wear a skirt, choose nude or skin tone complimentary hosiery. No fishnets or patterned tights.

In a professional setting it is best not to wear any facial jewelry such as nose, septum, lip, cheek, eyebrow, or chin piercings, or tongue rings. Review the company policy on wear of these items before your interview. When in doubt, leave them out.

5. Clothing for Men. A black or navy blue suit and tie is best, with a white buttoned-down shirt, matching belt and dress shoes. Next would be black or dark blue slacks with a white buttoned-down shirt and tie, with matching belt and loafers.

The last look is what I call "dockers casual," which is black or blue Dickies pants or khaki dockers, and a white buttoned-down shirt, or white polo shirt.

Make sure your clothing is free of wrinkles and excess lint; clip any threads hanging from suit jacket or pants hem with scissors or a nail clipper. Threads can also be carefully burned off with a lighter.

Try your pants on with the shoes you will be wearing to the interview to make sure the pants are not too long in the back, and have at least a slight break in the crease when resting on top of the shoe.

Wear dark or neutral socks. Wipe and polish your shoes removing visible scuff marks and excess debris, and make sure your shoe soles are intact.

6. Clothing for Women. A black or navy blue suit with a white buttoned-down shirt, or boat/scoop neck blouse or shell top. The suit can be with either a skirt or slacks. Next would be black or

dark blue slacks with a white or neutral buttoned-down shirt or boat/scoop neck blouse or shell top.

Lastly, is what I call "dockers casual" which is black or blue Dickies pants, or khaki dockers (or skirt), and a white neutral buttoned-down blouse, shell top, or polo shirt.

Make sure your clothing is free of wrinkles and excess lint; clip any threads hanging from your suit jacket or pants hem. Try your slacks on with the interview pair of shoes to make sure they are not too long in back, and have at least a slight break in the crease when resting on top of the shoe or foot.

Wear dark or neutral socks or hosiery. Shoes should be black, dark blue, or nude flats, loafers, or low-heeled pumps. Wipe and polish your shoes removing visible scuff marks and excess debris, and make sure your soles and heels are intact.

If you are financially challenged thrift stores are a great resource to find interview clothing. You can also try clothing consignment shops where you can trade other types of clothes and shoes for cash, then turn around and purchase the clothing you need for your interview.

Lastly, there are non-profit agencies that can assist you with finding job interview clothing and shoes. Now that your visual presentation is taken care of, let us move on to actual interview preparation.

Interviewing 101

A job interview is the ability to use your knowledge at the right time. ~ unknown

I strongly recommend conducting research before your interview. Find out everything you can about the company its leadership team, and any upcoming plans for the company's future. Research any scandals or negative publicity to see how it was handled, and whether positive changes were made.

Check the company website for any ethics policies, mission or vision statements, community, and social responsibility. Make sure the company's values and ethics are compatible with your own, else it may be challenging to work there, should you be asked to do something that goes against your personal moral code.

Go to the interview location the day before to make sure you know how much time you will need to get there, and to make sure there is no new construction or re-routes causing you to get lost and end up arriving late.

The day of your interview before you go into the room, take one to two deep breaths to calm any nervousness. Once inside the interview room be sure to greet everyone with a smile and a firm handshake.

There is nothing worse than a limp half-handed handshake. On the other hand (pun intended), do not try to break the interviewer's hand by gripping too tightly. A gentle squeeze and one to two up and down motions is sufficient.

Once you are seated you can place your hands on the table cupped together or rest them in your lap. Cross your legs at the ankle or sit with both feet flat on the floor. Sit near the edge of your seat to help you sit up straight. You want to be comfortably engaged, but not too relaxed by leaning back in the chair.

If water is offered, take a couple of sips to prevent dry mouth, and remove any gum or candy before speaking. You do not want gum flying out of your mouth or to choke on gum or candy mid-sentence, or to be "popping" and "cracking" gum in between answering questions.

When the interviewer asks a question, make eye contact with him or her while answering. If there is more than one interviewer, make eye contact with the person who asked the question, then look to each of the others as you respond.

Remember to use the interviewer(s) names when answering; "Great question, Sam, let me tell you how I..." Another way to standout while interviewing is to include the company mission into your response, using your own words.

If you are completely stumped by a question, be honest and state, "I am not familiar with that information at this time, but I will find out and get back to you."

If you remember the information during the interview, thank them for their patience and ask permission to readdress the question.

Most interviews end with, "Do you have any questions for me/us?" Always have at least two to three questions ready to ask the interviewer(s). Do your research on the company and ask mindful questions that will get more than a yes or no response.

For example, "What best practices have come from each company since the merger?" Other questions to ask include how long the interviewer has been with the company and what he or she likes best about working there.

You can also ask the interviewer(s) when they plan to make the final hiring decision. Lastly, ask for feedback on how they think your interview went, to identify opportunities for improvement should you have to interview again.

At the conclusion of the interview, "thank, shake, and take." Thank the interviewer(s) for the opportunity and any feedback they provided, shake hands, and ask for (take) business cards so you can send them individual "Thank You" notes or e-mails.

A "Thank You" note or e-mail may seem like an outdated practice however, when I began working at my last employer I found my "Thank You" note pinned to my new boss's bulletin board.

Sometimes you might be neck and neck with another candidate and the deciding factor could come down to who sent a "Thank You" note!

If there is a question you did not know the answer to during the interview, research it, and include the answer in your "Thank You" note response.

Sometimes a second or third interview is required. Stay ready! The final interview is usually with the person you will be working with daily. This interview is merely to see if you will get along personality-wise, and whether you will be a good fit with his or her team.

Potential Interview Questions

1. Tell us about yourself as it pertains to your work history?

2. What do you know about our organization?

3. Describe the most difficult working relationship you have had? What did you do to improve the relationship? What was the outcome?

4. What do you consider your professional strengths? Give a specific example using this attribute in the workplace.

5. What do you consider your greatest career achievement?

6. Please give an example of how you have supported diversity during your career.

7. If there comes a time during your workday where there is no work to be done, what would you spend that free time doing?

8. What excites you about this job opportunity?

9. What do you consider your professional weakness and what have you done to overcome it?

10. What qualifications do you possess that make you a better candidate for this position above anyone else?

Negotiating Pay

"Never split the difference."
~ Chris Voss

You rarely get paid what you are worth; you get paid what you negotiate for. It is crucial that you research what the current industry pay scale is nationally and in your local area. Knowing industry pay scale will be vital to your salary negotiation when the time comes.

Be prepared to justify why you are worth what you are asking for in salary, and be willing to negotiate* company stock, health benefits, and paid time off in lieu of cash compensation.

Should an interviewer mention salary or inquire as to what salary you are looking for, smile and request to reserve that discussion for once you have been hired. If they continue to press, having previously done your research, reiterate why you are the most qualified for the position, then state your desired salary.

*Lesson Learned: I had been out of work for several months when I interviewed and was selected for an Administrative Assistant position. The HR professional stated the salary and did not make it *sound* like the offer was negotiable. I accepted it because *I felt* I was near desperate for work.

After being in the position a few weeks I learned they were willing to pay me two thousand dollars more, than what was initially offered had I only negotiated!

My advice to you is to know your worth. Never let your current circumstances dictate your salary and always ask for *at least* two thousand dollars more than what you are willing to accept!

Even if you are offered more than you anticipated, still ask if the offer is negotiable. All they can say is "No" however, if they agree you have just given yourself a minimum two thousand dollar starting bonus! Get excited!

Some companies offer a salary increase after a ninety-day probationary period, but this not readily advertised or mentioned during interviews or salary negotiations. If a ninety-day salary bump is not mentioned, ask if the company has this policy and if so, ask to be considered for it once you are hired.

Congratulations!
You Got the Job. Now What?

"Remember to celebrate milestones as you prepare for the road ahead." ~ Nelson Mandela

Congratulations! You killed your interview, earned the position, and garnered the salary you negotiated for! I am so proud of you! I knew you could do it! High-five, fist-bump, and give yourself a pat on the back! Success looks good on you!

Take a minute to enjoy this victory. How does it feel? Who can you share this moment with? Who will celebrate your accomplishment with you? How will you celebrate? Great! Now go do it, then come back and we will go on to your next steps.

Hopefully, you gave yourself a few days to transition before starting work. Whether you gave two weeks' notice or whether you have been at home for several months, you will still need to adjust to a new routine so give yourself a few days to celebrate, then plan your new normal before you start working.

Some things to consider: your work wardrobe, daily commute and parking; whether to pack your lunch or frequent the company cafeteria, or which local restaurants near your new job deliver.

Other considerations are: How will you decorate your desk or cubby? What office supplies will you need if they are not already provided? And most importantly, what coffee mug will you use to introduce yourself to your new co-workers. Aah, concerns of the newly employed! Again, congratulations.

In our brief time together, I have shared with you what I believe are valuable and insightful tools for you to propel yourself forward, into your next career endeavor.

I hope my examples and lessons learned have been beneficial to you and/or showed you what *not* to do, or gave you confidence to take the next step in your professional journey.

Consider the Possibilities

"If money were no object and you knew you couldn't fail, what would you be doing?"
~ Alan Watts

The above quote is something that I ask each person who hires me to work on their resume. Their answer helps me to uniquely tailor their document. It is an uncanny method but it is my niche, and what works for me in helping others. I challenge you to answer the question for yourself as you build your own resume.

If you can answer the question, I believe you are headed in the direction of your destiny. Even if you still have to for a time, work for the money, know that someday you will be able to do what you love without money being a factor. This can motivate you to reach your destiny sooner.

If you cannot answer the question right away, spend some time thinking about what your life would look like if you could do the thing that quickens your spirit, ignites your passion for service, and brings a smile to your face. Consider the possibilities. That is all. Thank you.

Endorsements

"A compliment is verbal sunshine."
~ Robert Orben

"As a young adult, having a good resume is imperative to getting my foot in the door. Ms. Jackson's resume writing and tips on marketing myself have always done that for me, even for positions I was not fully qualified for."
C. Witherspoon, Tech Support II, Charter Communications

"I don't like to read but the opening story drew me in and I wanted to know more."
K. Johnson, Entrepreneur

"Whether you are changing careers or reentering the workforce, it is rare to find a how-to guide that not only prepares you for success but simplifies it in very practical ways. I personally benefitted from this jewel by receiving an offer after only two interviews! Not only that, but I negotiated my salary well above what I thought I could get. "The Resume Doctor" is a must if you are looking for an easy, yet helpful read."

K. Walker, Retired U.S. Air Force Technical Sergeant and newly hired civilian Executive Assistant

"Leslie's book is captivating. She provides a wealth of knowledge, advice, and tools to keep you inspired and help you evolve."
M. Shell, Chief Master Sergeant,
U.S. Air Force, Retired

"If she does your resume, you will get the job! Leslie is brilliant with making the things you do every day seem/read as fascinating."
T. Gilliam Family Nurse Practitioner

References and Resources

Frequently Asked Questions. (n.d.). Retrieved from usajobs.gov: https://www.usajobs.gov/Help/faq/application/documents/resume/what-to-include/

Maxwell, J. C. (2007). Maxwell Daily Reader: 365 Days of Insight to Develop the Leader Within You and Influence Those Around You. In J. C. Maxwell, Maxwell Daily Reader: 365 Days of Insight to Develop the Leader Within You and Influence Those Around You (p. 409). Nashville: Yates & Yates.

Vojinovic, I. (2019, Sep 10). 70 Recruitment Statistics for Attracting Top Talent in 2020. Retrieved from smallbizgenius: https://www.smallbizgenius.net/by-the-numbers/recruitment-statistics/#gref

Websites for Career Choices:

www.ncda.org

www.careeronestop.org

Clothing Resources: Clothes Mentor, Plato's Closet, your local thrift stores

www.dressforsuccess.org

All quotes were found via Google.com

About the Author

Leslie L. Jackson is a retired US Air Force Veteran who hails from Kansas City. She is a career Executive Administrator with over 30 years of military and civilian experience. Leslie has an Associate of Applied Science in Information Resources Management, a Bachelor of Science Degree in Human

Resources Development, and a Small Business Management Certification. She has three young adult daughters and currently resides in Norfolk, Virginia, where she enjoys sunrise walks on the bay, smooth jazz, travelling, chocolate, and all things purple. Leslie is also a published author of two children's books, *Treasures from Heaven* and *Melodies from Heaven.*

Made in United States
Troutdale, OR
02/29/2024

18055375R00040